WONDERMAN'S POETRY

POEMS OF HEALING

WONDERMAN37Z

America Star Books

First printing

America Star Books has allowed this work to remain exactly as the author intended, verbatim, without editorial input.

Softcover 9781611027549
PUBLISHED BY AMERICA STAR BOOKS, LLLP
www.americastarbooks.com

Printed in the United States of America

CROSSROAD

Each of us are on a crossroad to choose which are road to take.
Are we going to choose the road that lead toward worldly.
Or are we going to choose the road that will lead to Christ.
It is your choice, but I have chosen the road toward Christ.
For I want to be able to praise him and worship him in heaven.
I want my life in the end to be meaningful and beautiful.
One that other true believers will be able to say yes he belong to Christ

JESUS

Jesus, you are our source, you are our portion.
So we will not fear, for you are Awesome God.
We will chose to follow you through everything.
Because there is nothing that can separate us.
We will choose to walk the narrow path to the finish line.
There is nothing nor anyone that separate us.
You know all, so no one can lie to you about us.
You know our decisions and heart already Lord.

SAVIOR

O God you have rescue us, from a death that is worst.
You have not only spoke our healing into existence.
But you took the brut of our suffering upon your shoulders.
You gave your life, for our lives and rescue us from doom.
A death that we deserve, because of the sins that we have done.
So we give you our praise and honor you with true worship.
For you took a death, that you did not deserve to rescue us.
From the death that we have really deserve, thank you God.

FAITH

When you have the faith, you can heal the sick.
When you trust with your complete heart Jesus.
That God will save you from your current situation.
Then it will happen maybe not the way you expect.
But it shall happen the way that Christ wants it to be.
For his thoughts are not like our thoughts, they are better.
So when Christ does deliver you from it, it shall be better.
For he already see how it will come about in your life./
So trust him for he loves you and will never hurt you

SPIRITUAL

Hello, Trust Christ for he will never leave nor abandon you, never.
Stand firm, do not budge the strength of the Lord is always yours.
Run to God when temptation seems too fierce to overcome on your own.
Never fight on your own understanding but allow the Spirit to guide you.
For Christ sent his Spirit, to help and to teach us how remain victorious.
So pray, read your bible and trust in Christ on everything you go through.
Follow Christ, obey him and let him guide you to wherever you need to be.
When you see the world sinning, pray for each of them to find God too.

WANTED

Believers with open hearts ready to lay down your life for your God.
Long hours, with blessings beyond your wildest imaginations.
Miracles happening every day, but you must die to self everyday.
Trusting that your heavenly Father will protect you from harm.
That he will bring you back from the dead, to live a joyful life in heaven.
If this seems like a perfect fit for you apply to Jesus in a prayer.
He will definitely let you know, if you have gotten the position

HELP CHANGE ME

We the body of Christ never compromise our relationship with Christ.
For he must always come first, for he is our best friend and source of life.
So if you are compromising your relationship with him, better be careful.
Ask for forgiveness and then repent for he should be your everything.
For Christ is good, all the time, no one else even comes close.
I know that sometimes our hearts wanders because of our brokenness.
When this stuff happens, cry out to Christ ask him to heal you.
For if you truly are sincere, about being his disciple and child.
He will never leave you nor forsake you as his child and best friend.

FOLLOWER

I am a follower of Christ, the living God.
My faith, he has been building on it.
I am just the man that he uses to write the poetry.
But it is Christ extra helping on the poetry.
I am so blessed that Christ loves me so much.
So I will praise him, and always worship him.
He is so Awesome, I thank you Lord Jesus.
For everything that you have done for me.

WORSHIP YOU

I give my all, as worship to you, O Living God.
I lay down my life, to worship you Lord Jesus.
There is only living a life of sacrifice to you.
For you are Holy God, I stand to worship you.
Take me as I am, I will worship you for you are good.
This life means nothing, I will worship you Jesus.
Heal me God, use all of me to show true worship of you
For I am nothing,, without you Lord I want to worship you.
In every part of my life, I want the world see

FOOLISH

What a sad pathetic existence that a lot live in.
For they are so consume by what they feel and need.
That they fail to see the hurting, Christ and everyone else.
They are so caught up in hording everything from everyone else.
You should be ashamed of yourself, this is not about you.
But it is about Christ, the creator of each of our very souls.
Who are you to think that the world evolves around you.
On judgment day, you will wish that you had heed my warning

GOD FORGIVENESS

O how dark this world is right now Family.
How I pray that this whole world would repent.
Then chase after the Christ, I pray this will happen.
But I also know what Jesus said himself to people.
That only a few would find the road that leads to Heaven.
But I am still praying that many will see the Light.
Thus repenting, thus being drawn to you O Holy One.
I have the faith that people that Christ has put in my path.
Shall not only be save, but healed and restored too.

YOU ARE PERFECT

Here we stand, to worship you Holy One of God.
There is none that are good except you, only you.
Your Grace which you have seal our salvation in.
You see all things, you have seen our end and beginnings.
So you alone are worthy to be praise and worship Lord.
I give all that I am to you O Holy God, only to you.
I fall upon my face, to worship you O Holy Savior.
For only you can save our souls, only you can rescue us.
So I give you my everything to transform into something beaut

OVERCOMING LIFE

There is only one way to overcome life's problems.
Through the Spirit of God which is the Holy Spirit.
Because we most of the time can not overcome them on our own.
But when we have the Holy Spirit living within us, we can.
But it is only because God is fixing our problems not us.
For I know that I am far from being a problem-solver.
But I know the creator whom created all of the good things.
He knows how to fix the problems because he created everything

EXTRAORDINARY

Normal is overrated, too many people are normal.
I on the other hand would rather be extraordinary.
Because by this I know the true Living God name Jesus.
He gives us his Spirit to dwell within us to help us.
To overcome the things that comes against us here.
The power of the Holy Spirit is quite extraordinary.
To overcome this word, the Holy Spirit will protect us.
The Holy Spirit also will show the world Christ.
Through us so that they shall have no excuse on Judgement day.

OVERCOME

O Savior, deliverer of my wasting life here.
Create in me strength to overcome my trials.
Teach me how to lay down my sins here.
For I want to be going to heaven after I pass away.
So do a mighty transforming inside of my life.
Rework my attitude, among my behavior too.
Transform me into your likeness Lord God.
Heal me, restore me, create in me a righteous heart.
Create in me a steadfast spirit, finish your work in me.

I WILL STAND

I will stand, not because I am strong nor am I brave.
But because you keep strengthening me, with your Spirit.
I will stand not because I am strong, or because I am brave.
Because I am quite weak, and am not ashamed to admit it.
I will soar, not because I can fly like a eagle soar.
But because I will be bless and spiritually empower by your spirit.
Which dwells within me through your Holy Spirit.
I shall overcome all obstacles thrown at me everyday.
Not because I am a super hero, but because you protect me.

I SHALL STAND

Whatever happen I must trust that its in your will.
For I know that you have everything under control.
So I must quit worrying over bad things happening.
For I must trust you, and lay my will down to pick up yours.
Because I do know that you love me and will be with me.
I must walk with the confident that you are protecting me.
While praising your most Worthy, and perfect name God.
So I will start walking like a overcome, not a coward.

GOD

Christ hear my plead, I need you to come to my rescue.
I need you to do a huge working in me, for I keep failing you.
I am not the strong perfect soldier that I need Lord God.
As much as you have reveal yourself to me, I should be.
I keep allowing my brokenness and hurts keep me,,
From being the strong warrior I should already be.
God heal me, so that I can stand strong on your word.
Bringing others out of this depressive life I am trap in.
I do know that you are my hope, my strength, and strong tower.
But I am still trap in this depression, over my failures.

FOREVER

We will die in this life, this is a promise unless Christ comes first.
Even then it depends on who side you are on whether you will die or not.
For revelation says that the lost shall battle Christ till he destroy them.
After all this time he is not coming as a pacifist, but as a warrior.
For right now we are called to love others as we love ourselves.
But once Christ comes the kid gloves shall be off and he will fight back.
The people will bring it on themselves because they took the mark.
They choose the side that they agree with and it was not the side of God.
They finally got off of the fence, and went to the losing side.

REDEMPTION

I whom once ran from obedience to you O God.
Now receives the redemption from you Lord.
For you freely give your redemption to people.
Whom once were disobedient to you Jesus.
You give us grace and mercies everyday.
Even though we really do not deserve them.
Yet you love us enough, and sees something within us.
That we have not seen in us yet, thank you God

BROKEN-HEARTED

Have you ever met the love of your life, the one whom is your soul-mate.
But then was told by Christ that you would never be them at all.
Have you ever been lead away from obedience to Christ Jesus.
By a person that you were connected with in every single way.
I met her the woman of my dream, the only one I ever truly love.
To have fallen into sin with her, when I should have been stronger.
But Christ forgives and always give his people second chances.
To become the people that he has created us to be in the beginning.

SURRENDERING

What do I have to lose, my life been turmoil as it is.
The struggling to stay above the waves of the storms.
Trusting that there is a purpose to these storms.
So I must keep moving on persevering in this life.
Staying to myself is very painful most of the time.
The ones that I want to see I do not see very much.
Knowing that this isolation will not last forever.
Trusting that there is a purpose behind this Lord God

YOUR LOVE

Your love is freely given and I freely accepted it.
Your love is everlasting and unconditional.
For you love me the way that I am God.
Your sent your spent to heal my pain and suffering.
You choose me to become your blessed child.
All that you have already done for me, thank you.
For you are a awesome Savior, Friend and God.
Blessed be you Mighty Name O Lord God.

RENEWAL

I have been renewal through the Living God.
My life has changed for the better through Christ.
He is my strength, my soul gets renewal through him.
He is my provider, my best friend, and my King.
When he draws me nearer, I am raise up by him.
He protects us from harm, and delivers me through hardships.
He walks me through the hardships then uses me to bring others out.
He is the Light that I see at the very end of the tunnel.

LIVING SUPERNATURAL

I am living supernatural, here on this planet of ours.
Because I have a Savior, whom is working through me.
I seen the many miracles that he has preform through me.
He has saved my life many of times more then I can remember.
He has blessed me too beyond all measures, for he is good.
He restores what is stolen from the evil one too.
He is my Lord, God, and Creator, that blesses me.
With long live and abundant blessings to go with it.
The poetry he writes through me to help others.

BROKEN

I may be broken, but through Christ I am invincible.
Just like an egg you have to break it shell to get on the inside.
We too have to become broken so people can see Christ in us.
So know when you become broken it can be use to help others.
Show them Christ within you, and the miracles that he preforms,
in your life everyday will draw them to him to help them too.
So that your poems can help heal other people too whom,
are going through now what you have already went through.
So stand tall, let God heal you and use you to heal others.

HEALING

When you came to me, you ask me what I needed.
Since I am very broken, you already knew this too.
So I said that I needed to be healed by you God.
So since then you been working on four things.
1 You are healing me, second you are delivery me.
Third, you have been working on building my faith.
The fourth and final thing is trusting you Lord.
Through it all the trust is the most important of all.
In all relationships are based on trusting the other person

POWERFUL LIFE

There is power in a life, laid down for others.
There is power in a life given over to Christ.
There is power in becoming a servant to all.
There is power through the Holy Spirit within.
To put others before yourself, thus leading by example.
Its easy to call yourself a Christian, but its much harder.
Following through with becoming a true Christian.
There is power not your own spirit but Christ Spirit,
That dwells within you is where the power comes from.

WHO AM I

Who am I to walk on water, while holding your hand Jesus.
Because like Peter if I let go then I will sink into the sea.
Who am I to walk on water, because I am no different then anyone else.
The only difference is that you have taken a special interest in me.
Because in truth I mess up every day, I am just blessed by Christ.
I am just a ordinary man who has connection with a supernatural God.
A God who promises are truth and he is always faithful to his people.
Who am I to walk on water, I am a son of the Most High God.

SALVATION

When Christ redeems you, he starts a good work in you.
When you truly belongs to him, he shall finish that work.
So be strong, never forget that Christ is still working on you.
So do not let that evil one make you feel lost or thrown to the curb.
For if Christ has save you, he will finish the job that he already startled.
Praise the Lord, for he is not like man leaving a job unfinished.
Just trust in God to finish the work inside of you, because he shall.
Then you shall bow before him when you see him and praise his worthy name.

THOUGH IT ALL

O Holy Creator, The Word, your words speak life into my soul.
Your words are healing vapor, healing my inner being always.
As dark as my life has been, your Light shines healing ray into it.
cleansing me of my addictions, sins, and most of all my attitude.
For you change people from the inside-out cleansing them.
Of everything that is not of you, thus we then resemble you God.
For you are always working cleansing and molding us too.

FREEDOM

I am free, because you have delivered me from sin.
This freedom is fantastic, I praise you for everything.
For the strength that you have empowered me with.
Though the Holy Spirit which is within me Lord.
You have empower us with so much, of your gifts.
In turn people shall see you within us daily Lord.
The testimonies are another gift you have empower us with.
Each trial that we go through will only make us stronger.
At the same point we are still living because of your protection

I DONT CARE

Lord I don't care what people think about my love for you.
There are a lot of fools in this world whom don't want to believe in you.
They enjoy sinning way too much, to want to give it up for you.
My love for you is real, I am not afraid to say I love you God.
You are everything to me, I have nothing but what you give to me.
I am blessed by you, I have what I need and that's enough.
My life is a blessed by you, its not always easy to live this life.
But through your strength, I get through it everyday God.

I LEARN

I learn in life Christ is always faithful, for he is always good too.
He will lift you up, if you keep your pride in check, he will bless you.
With his tender-mercies, and loving kindness too so stand firm.
But if pride sets in and you think that this is all about you.
Then you are going to fall, the Lord hates pride in anyone.
But the humble will be raise up, so never forget this child.
Always remember the world does not evolve around you.
It evolves around Christ Jesus alone, so humble yourself.

LOVE YOU LORD

I come to realize your Love is sweeter then wine.
You have saved me from death, here on this world.
Your love is sweeter then any woman's love could ever be.
Your love is sweeter then wine or the sweetest brownies.
Your love is the best, you whom have rescue Israel from death.
You have lead them out of Egypt, where they were held captive.
Rescuing them you lead them into their promise land you gave to them.
The land of milk and honey, they have became your chosen people.
So Lord God, I will always love you with a complete heart, you are my life.

INTENTISIONAL SACRIFICE

He live a life, destine for suffering bruise, batter through it all he still love.

Torture, beaten, robbed, yet he still was royalty not of this world though.

Even though he owned everything in sight, he could have call down his soldiers.

But then how could he become the sacrifice that he knew he was meant to be.

For only through this huge suffering, and sacrifice could he become a Savior.

To a group of people that were once his enemies, but now his best friends.

For only through his huge sacrifice would he show his love for us.

In a way as humans, that we would understand him clearly thank you Lord.

HEALER

I stand before you the Healer of my soul.
I fall upon my knees to worship you, my Healer.
For your ways are good, your ways are pure and holy.
I will worship you O God, for you are the Healer of my soul.
I will stand in Awe of you, for I have seen what you have done.
So I shall fall upon my face, to worship you O Lord God.
For you are so worthy, you are so good and awesome.

MY HOPE

There is but one true Hope of the world.
He was nailed to the cross over 2000 years ago.
Yes this world is getting darker as we speak.
But he can still save you, and use you to help others.
For he is all about love, Loving others unconditionally.
Putting others ahead of yourself, like he did when he walk the earth.
He put others before himself, like when he went to the cross.
Dying on it, so that we may have life through his sacrifice.

CHRIST LIGHT

There is but one Light which brings true Hope.
For most people crave the darkness to hide their deeds.
But when you step into the Light, your darkness revealed.
So stand in the Light allow it to shine through you always.
Thus revealing your deeds to this world are sincere.
Thus drawing people to your Gods throne room.
For then they too shall become children of the Light.
Leading the Lost, hopeless, and hurting into Gods Light too

MIRACLE

Christ has transform us into living Miracles.
All of the things that we have gone through.
To come out stronger, not being destroyed.
For many people have been destroyed by less.
Destroying themselves instead of persevering.
Which is what Christ has called us to do trust him.
Not give up on this life become overcomers here.
To not allow the evil one to deceive you into destruction.
But to stand firm and fast, to become overcomers in life.

MERCY

If we were judge on our sins, we would all be headed to hell.
But instead we are judge on our relationship and faith too.
For once we start to build a relationship with Christ Jesus.
He starts to build up the faith that we shall need to overcome.
Which will be like a boulder going down a snow mountain.
Building a speed that will make it zoom much faster down
This is how faith is built too it is built up to zoom.
Its not us that builds up faith but its Christ works in us.

REDEEM

Redeem from the sins that I have done in the past.
Redeem to become a true child of the Living God.
Redeem from my rebelliousness and attitudes.
Redeem from a life that was wasted till now.
Redeem from being just a another member of the crowd.
Redeem from living a selfish, non sacrificial life here.
Redeem to fight for the fatherless, widows, and poor.
Redeem to be the child that you have created me to be.

I AM

I am a child of the living God name Jesus Christ.
I am a new creation in him, one full of grace and faith.
I am all that Christ has called me to become in the new life.
I am healed, I am restored, and I am safe under his wings.
I am his son, not a stranger but a family member of Gods.
I am a strong spiritual warrior through Christ Jesus.
I am a doer of his word not a failure but a Overcomer.
I am here because Christ has called me out of the darkness.
I am here because he has brought me into the light of his love.

THANK YOU

O Holy one, my redeemer and very best friend.
After looking over my past life in a clear view.
Seeing your faithfulness at every single turn.
Knowing that even through the very dark times.
There was a purpose on why you allow them.
I see your finger prints in all of the good things.
So I just want you to know that I am very grateful.
I want to thank you for everything that you did.

TIME

Its time to get serious with Christ, for soon he shall appear.
To get his children and take us to the heavens above us.
Then there will be a dark time here on this planet earth.
Where people shall suffer because of the evil satan.
His people then will be in constant danger of death.
Because at this time evil shall reign on this planet.
But fear not for our God is still in control over things.
So rejoice and praise his most worthy name.

HEALED

We are healed by our faith, once we know the truth.
That Christ heals those whom believe in it, it will be done.
For faith is a seed that is planted in our minds by what we believe.
Christ will heal you through your faith in the truth that he is love.
So trust in his love for you, believe that he has healed you already.
Thank him for all that he has done in your lives today and always.
But most important, know that he is God and God alone.
For he speaks everything good into existence, for he is Good

FAST LIVES

We are like vapors, here today and gone tomorrow.
But that is this life alone, our next life is forever.
To live with Christ throughout all eternality is awesome.
A life where we can show Christ our love face to face.
Let him see that we love him unconditionally too.
For our love for him shall be exactly liker his love for us.
We shall have a sinless body once we make it to heaven.
No more suffering, anger, sin just unconditional love.

I SEE CHRIST

I see Christ in the moonlight, the sunlight, in the rainbows,
and in the stars.
In everything that is free, I see Christ in the beauty of nature,
in the sky.
For how else can they be woven and blend in the most perfect
of ways.
Unless Christ whom is God the son whether you believe or
not created it.
How else could life come about on this, planet that we all live
on, then die on.
Unless there is truly a Savior that spoke us all into existence
out of nothing.
I seen God in everything that he has created into existence, for
he is Awesome.
So I will stand in awe to give him the honor and praise that he
deserves

THE LOVE OF A SAVIOR

The love of a savior, is what the whole world is looking for.
Most are called by him but only a few are chosen by him.
Really it does not matter the gender, because it is a family love.
Not the kind of love sought after here on the planet earth.
God is Holy, beyond that of mortal men and women.
He is the creator and parent to us all, we will be brothers,,,
Sisters, and he shall be our Father, thank you Abba Daddy.
Jesus shall be our older awesome brother, I think you Lord.
So we are super blessed to have the love of a Savior.
For God so love the world, that he gave his begotten son.
That whomever believes in him shall not perish but have eternal life.

CHRIST LOVE

Your love for me leaves me breathless and in awe.
In the morning, I, talk with you, in the evening.
I praise your most worthy name my Savior.
For your beauty is so Awesome my Savior.
I love you Lord Jesus, you are everything to me.
I am not ashamed to say just how much I adore you.
Your Love is sweeter then the most sweetest cake.
I will forever worship you my Lord and King.
Thank you fort saving my life, and my soul.

FOREVER FAITHFUL

Holy one, here I come to worship you.
For you are Worthy, you are Holy.
Here I come to bow before your throne.
To sing praises to my worthy Savior.
I am lost without you God, I am yours.
You are Awesome, you are my Savior.
There are no other as Awesome as you.
There is only you, my Lord and God.
So I shall bow before you O Holy On